T0208343

I FLOW

*738+ Words Toward Awareness
and Mental Freedom*

FLAVIA MOSCI, M.S.

BALBOA.
PRESS
A DIVISION OF HAY HOUSE

This book is a work of non-fiction. Unless otherwise noted, the author and the publisher make no explicit guarantees as to the accuracy of the information contained in this book and in some cases, names of people and places have been altered to protect their privacy.

Balboa Press books may be ordered through booksellers or by contacting:

Balboa Press
A Division of Hay House
1663 Liberty Drive
Bloomington, IN 47403
www.balboapress.com
1 (877) 407-4847

Because of the dynamic nature of the Internet, any web addresses or links contained in this book may have changed since publication and may no longer be valid. The views expressed in this work are solely those of the author and do not necessarily reflect the views of the publisher, and the publisher hereby disclaims any responsibility for them.

The author of this book does not dispense medical advice or prescribe the use of any technique as a form of treatment for physical, emotional, or medical problems without the advice of a physician, either directly or indirectly. The intent of the author is only to offer information of a general nature to help you in your quest for emotional and spiritual well-being. In the event you use any of the information in this book for yourself, which is your constitutional right, the author and the publisher assume no responsibility for your actions.

Any people depicted in stock imagery provided by Getty Images are models, and such images are being used for illustrative purposes only. Certain stock imagery © Getty Images.

Print information available on the last page.

ISBN: 978-1-9822-3119-4 (sc)
ISBN: 978-1-9822-3124-8 (e)

Library of Congress Control Number: 2019909565

Balboa Press rev. date: 07/27/2019

Get serious about yourself, your life and who you want to become!

I flow is an innovative method that provides a foundation with building blocks to support you in removing your limitations and in channeling your inner forte!

DEDICATION

To my readers: Time to get serious about yourself, your life and who you want to become! I flow is an innovative method that provides a foundation with building blocks to support you in removing your limitations and in channeling your inner forte! My hope is that this foundation will help you as much as it has helped me throughout my journey.

To my sister, Gabi Mosci who has always inspired me to believe that anything is possible. To my parents Silvia and Ricardo Mosci who have been the best mentors and role models I could have wished for, and who taught me the meaning of unconditional love. Thank you for teaching me to believe in myself, in God and in my dreams. To my nephew Lennox, who is the biggest blessing that has come into our lives. It is amazing how a 4-year-old can teach us about gratitude, he has this wonderful way of appreciating every little nice thing that happens around him, and he expresses it in such a cute way that it always puts a smile in our face. Andrei Tudor Patrascu, thank you for all your feedback while I was completing my work, you inspired me in many ways. To my professors, supervisors, and mentors who have had a great amount of influence in my journey : Dr. Miles Matise, Dr. Abby Hall, Dr. Anita Pembleton, Stephen Notari, Kaitlyn Abadia. Thanks to Lunapic.com for cover photo editing. Thank you! I am very grateful to all of you...

CONTENTS

CHAPTER 1

What's in a Problem?

> Man is not worried by real problems so much as by his imagined anxieties about real problems.
>
> - Epictetus

Ah ... those persistent thoughts that do not seem to go away, regardless of our attempts to rationalize with them! They manage to draw the life right out of us. We all experience problems and challenges throughout our lives—that is a part of being human. We cannot completely stop obstacles from coming our way. But at times, it seems that some of our problems can become downright stubborn, leaving us feeling completely stuck. At first sight, their intensity may seem to be merely attributable to the situation itself (the external factors), whether it be related to work, finances, school, a relationship, health, or something else. But if we were to take a closer look, we might discover that it is our own thinking about the problem that usually adds all the heavy weight. If you always find yourself in a repeating situation, with the same problem showing up over and over again, it would be wise to question your patterns of thinking that may be trapping you in that circle. Some of our negative patterns can share some very common features; they may be bursting with drama and shakeups and causing plenty of dysfunctions in our daily lives. These negative and challenging thought patterns keep running and interacting in the background, almost as if they have a mind of their own.

At times we try and fail repeatedly in our attempts to improve the situation at hand. This leaves us feeling drained and hopeless, and, at times, paralyzed. That very point at which we become overwhelmed by our unproductive, nagging thoughts is when we begin to stall. At the climax of a tug of war between our beliefs, thoughts, feelings, and behavior, the solution of the problem tends to remain obscure.

When our minds pull us in one direction and our hearts and beliefs reflect something else, our feelings tend to become unbalanced.

As a matter of fact, our own feelings could become so out of control, that we may even attempt to blame them for being the original cause of the problem. While constantly exhausting ourselves with persistent negative feelings, we then become unable to trust our own judgement and our decision-making abilities.

With so much confusion and loss of confidence, eventually we end up giving our power away completely. We lose our ability to effectively direct our own paths. We also lose hope and turn fatalistic, as if nothing we can do would ever produce a change. We withdraw from our daily lives and declare ourselves unable to properly handle even the simplest issues. This is exactly what happens when we are being held hostage by the patterns and content of our limited and negative thinking.

CHAPTER 2

Fear Tries to Interfere

At this point we may want to understand the origin of our negative rationale. The way by which we construct our version of reality takes into consideration information reported by our senses. This information gets interpreted by various internal processes, while we attempt to generate appropriate meaning. What we initially perceive gets filtered through our memory bank and is influenced by its beliefs and associated emotions. Finally, it gets categorized and stored into pre-existing "files" belonging to specific themes.

It is very important to remember that our belief system has a long history and has been shaped for all those years by a multitude of internal and external factors throughout our lives, such as our personal experiences, family, society, support system, environment, self-concept, motivation, individual role requirements, educational background, worldview, social and economic backgrounds, and religion. What happens when a new scenario is perceived through the eyes of our long-held beliefs? All these dynamics play a tremendous role in shaping the meanings that have been stored.

Now let's talk about some of the adverse experiences that you may have had in life. Given the unpleasantness of certain emotions caused by negative past experiences, a platform of negative thoughts usually forms around them. These groups of old, stored thoughts and beliefs, along with their related emotions, will then constantly compete for our attention in the present, each time we are faced with a situation that has the smallest resemblance to the old one. Consequently, this takes away our ability to clearly evaluate the current situation.

Imagine, if you will, that annoying computer pop-up that keeps blocking the screen you would like to access. These pop-ups appear in places they don't really belong to. I see some automatic thoughts working in such ways.

There is a problem when the content of our memory bank has been sealed with so many painful experiences, or even just one traumatic event. The wounded mind can be a terrifying experience.

Those emotionally charged memories can critically distort the lenses through which we currently filter out new information, and as this happens, those correlated negative emotions are experienced all over again. So now you may ask, what keeps us tied to our past negative beliefs and experiences? Why does our mind always go running back to them for opinion?

Fear. Fear is what takes us back. Fear is a common bond holding most past negative experiences, and it is always on high alert. It is one of the most powerful forces in life.

Fear behaves as an alarm system screaming things such as, "Watch out!" "Be careful!" "Don't trust!" "You will fail again!" "You are not enough!" "You are not smart enough!" "You don't deserve!" "You look terrible!" "No one loves you!" "You are weak!" "You are a looser!" "You are ugly!" "You are defected!" "You can't do this!" This list could go on indefinitely. These, of course, are just a few of the many themes through which fear likes to hides.

What is fear? Fear is conceived to be an evolutionary step toward our survival, as it keeps us primed in the face of danger. It serves its purpose. Fear can be perceived by us as being physical or emotional. The problem appears when fear becomes irrational and distorts the accuracy of our perception. Fear can lead us to make unrelated and erratic associations while we are interpreting reality. The fear memories that we have experienced in the past tend to linger; these recollections can be strong, defiant, and resistant. In many circumstances fear can cause havoc in our lives. It can be paralyzing. Furthermore, not only does it affect our present choices, it can be quite demanding and impose its dogmas on all our future expectations. When you focus on the worst possible outcome, you actually live it. A fearful mind can take thoughts and turn them into emotional experiences. It will not necessarily differentiate whether your fear is imagined or not. But keep in mind that most of our fears have been learned. Just remember—when you have a fear, you have a choice. There are ways to escape being held hostage by them.

CHAPTER 3

Congruency through Purpose

Now is the time to get serious about living your ideals.

- Epictetus

To live a life of virtue, match up your thoughts, words, and deeds.

- Epictetus

A second element keeping our negativity and conflicts alive is the lack of an ultimate purpose in life. Congruence of feelings, beliefs, thoughts, and behavior can only genuinely be achieved when our higher purpose has been clearly defined. An ultimate goal can provide us with the essential structure, as it sets priorities that keep us from losing sight of what is important in life. Without an ultimate vision, we may lose perspective. A clearly defined sense of purpose serves as a blueprint for thoughts, emotions, and behavior, providing them with a point of reference from which we can base our life's decisions. It is particularly important because a purpose keeps all variables in harmony. A well-defined purpose allows for clear intent. What is your purpose in this life? What are your passions and dreams?

It is important now, in order to understand the next concept, to examine the various functions of a thought.

CHAPTER 4

To Think About Our Thinking

Instead of talking about what thoughts are, let us first examine what thoughts do. With thoughts we perceive, analyze, and interpret the events and situations in our lives. It is through our thoughts that we express ideas, problem solve, and basically assert our realities. Our thoughts can inspire, nurture, comfort, and heal. Unfortunately, the opposite is also true: certain thoughts can simply destroy us and take us into a dark place. What we understand about the world, we understand from the perspective of our thoughts. Our future is essentially dependent upon our current thinking. It is by means of our thoughts that we are able to express our inner selves and communicate with our inner and outer worlds.

And most importantly, our thoughts color our emotions, shape our behavior, and help us define our beliefs. They depict our past, structure our present, and outline our future. That is quite a responsibility! I think you get the picture. Our thoughts are not us; they are a part of us. With all of this in mind, let me ask you two questions: What are the current themes running through your thoughts? Who is managing them?

This brings us to the third problem, which is not realizing that we have power over our thinking. Did you ever stop for a minute to examine your thoughts? Through the process of thinking, what we are essentially doing is managing all types of internal and external data.

We tend to think that our minds run on auto-play because we fail to see the connection between input and outflow. Understandably so, as much of the processing happens outside our level of awareness—that is, it incorporates preconscious and subconscious elements. But these need not to remain outside our plane of awareness, because at any given point, we are presented with an opportunity to discover, re-evaluate and revise our programming.

We tend to think of the acts of perceiving and interpreting as being passive processes, but in truth, they are quite the opposite. Our feelings and sensations by themselves are unable to provide a unique description of the world around us; they must be given meaning, and that is the part where you must be actively involved. In order to convey meaning to a new situation, we usually turn to our past experiences for comparison. We must understand that sometimes solving new problems in the same way as we did in the past may not work. There are no two situations that are ever exactly the same. We must be able to confront new situations with a new set of eyes. Remember, even the resources available in the now are different than the resources available back then. For this reason, we must free ourselves of our misconceptions by constantly updating our thinking program.

Don't be deceived! Thoughts should not just happen to you— pay more attention! The content and quality of your thoughts can be improved. Our thoughts need constant cleansing and renewal. Remember that thinking is only as passive as you want it to be, and for changes to happen, you must become the thinker in action. You must be able to examine and decide whether your current themes are working toward your goals, survival, and well-being. You decide the focus, and that creates the feelings and actions. Pay good attention because all this negative thinking can eventually give rise to a variety of ills: anxiety, depression, despair, hopelessness. Some thought patterns can dangerously increase our stress levels, consequently weakening our immune system and predisposing us to many illnesses. If we want to experience comfort, joy, healing, and peace, our thoughts need to reflect such themes. By systematically improving the content of your thoughts, you will notice that they will start working in your favor.

Be in charge! This is the goal. You are responsible for what you do with your thoughts.

CHAPTER 5

The Power of Our Self-Concept

I want to bring up a very important subject: Let's talk about self-love, self-worth, and self-care. Our self-concept directly influences our interpretations, as well as our expectations. If you are lacking in any one of these areas, you might already be running into a lot of issues in your life. Negative thoughts originating from these areas could possibly be keeping you locked in a circle of negative emotions and beliefs. If we are coming from a healthy and nurturing background, where our parents or our principal caregivers provided us with all of these things, naturally we grew up learning how to develop those within ourselves. As we mature from being that needy child to a healthy, developed adult, we learn the skills to comfort, nurture, and love ourselves. We grow to become our own emotional providers, caretakers, and motivators through life. Within that process we also learn to trust, respect, and value ourselves and our abilities. If initially those have been neglected, and we have not been provided with these essential models, the transition may not take place properly, and a very undeveloped self can arise. One can then become an adult who is constantly trying to get self-assurance from the outside world. If we do not learn our roles as self-providers of comfort and confidence, we will always be relying on others to gratify our fragile egos. We will constantly expect others to make us feel good about ourselves in order to feel happy and confident, and this can be plain right unproductive and exhausting.

When we create unsound expectations and impose them on other people in order to fill our emotional gaps, we usually end up in disappointment. Also, when we lack self-love and have low self-worth, we begin to misinterpret other people's actions, in a very similar manner to the one reflecting our poor beliefs. The absence of self-love leaves us very vulnerable, and it keeps us in a constant search for negative confirmations. We micro-focus and only look to see what we believe is already true; we will look for and find every instance to construct that reality that love is a lack, while we set out to illustrate how others do not love and value us. We will spend our lives selectively searching for negative feedback, so as to continue to convince ourselves that we are unlovable and unworthy. This simply reaffirms our negative beliefs, and so they continue to gather strength and grow exponentially. Unfortunately, as this cycle continues, all sorts of negative emotions linger around, and our thinking remains in this eternal loop.

CHAPTER 6

What Causes This Faulty System?

For many years, I was myself guilty of harboring a lot of negative thoughts. I struggled with high stress levels, anxiety, panic attacks, rumination, and chronic illness. Many times I felt completely hopeless. I can tell you now that my unbending patterns had kept me from experiencing full joy in my life, especially in my relationships with loved ones. My feelings were not always congruent with my logical thinking, and this amplified my indecision and anxiety. Many times I found myself making justifications in order to explain my emotions away. My fears of making the proper changes, due to my negative anticipation of outcomes, kept me trapped in unproductive situations. I began not to trust my own judgement. I felt as though I was constantly juggling negative thoughts and emotions, while I remained frozen.

These patterns that I discovered in myself seemed to run deeper. For the first time I began to notice my negative self-talk; this talk was discouraging, needy, and time-consuming. What was important at that point, though, was that something major took place: my awareness of it all. I decided at the time to write down all of my negative thoughts. As I set out to pinpoint each one of them, I realized they had a self-amplifying quality. As I tried to restrain one of these thoughts, I noticed that a stronger one would unexpectedly emerge in another area. The more I resisted a thought, the more it intensified. Ignoring them was not that simple, and it did not work.

I later realized that each negative emotion that I was experiencing was actually being shared by many different past experiences and beliefs, and not just by one, two, or a few thoughts.

Our memories are a part of a complex system. New data and information do not travel down a single straight path; they do not follow a linear process of storage. What they do instead is look for all the stored memories that may share similarities, whether in emotions, outcomes, or matching data. They then try to assimilate with those elements. This new information adheres to all the areas where it is welcomed. In essence, what we store are themes and meanings, not just a series of standalone data. Think, if you will, of your mind as a gigantic library. Within this library, the emotions are the reference labels that open up a world of experiences and beliefs. When you open a book, you will find thousands of thoughts and events related within. Those books are themed by some of your core beliefs.

Take the feeling of hopelessness, for example. Imagine that today you arrive at work only to receive the message from your supervisor that your job is being replaced. You panic. While you drive home, your mind begins to reinforce your feeling of hopelessness by presenting you with all the old supporting evidence from memory. Each event from the past that you begin to remember as sharing even the slightest resemblance will serve only to amplify this feeling, validating it even more. Old thoughts and beliefs can dramatically enhance the perception of danger related to a situation at hand.

It is not hard to find many instances in which you have felt hopeless throughout your life. Even unrelated information may mistakenly have been attached to it. Any experience slightly resembling a past one could be inappropriately used to reinforce current negative emotions. The subject of psychological and biological mental processes is still under scientific debate. Currently, we do not have a definite map illustrating how data get processed, stored, and retrieved. What we can certainly observe is that patterns and connections within our mind are highly interconnected.

Let us look at another example: the belief that no one really likes us. Your partner tells you that they feel more comfortable if you do not accompany them on their trip to visit their parents. Your first feeling would be, perhaps, one of rejection and sadness. A thought may pop up to remind you of an instance when a group of kids refused to play with you in preschool. You look around, and you compare your deprived social life to that of your colleagues; you think to yourself, "No one does like my company." More memories surface to remind you of all the rejection you experienced throughout your life. This new situation can now trigger the memory of all the previous ones, serving only to amplify your misery and feeling of being unloved. "That is it!" you say to yourself. You have now selectively found plenty of confirmation.

Now set aside the ego and the fear for a moment. What if, in reality, your partner wanted to spare you some of the stress of having to resolve extended family conflicts? What if they were actually trying to love you and protect you from added turmoil? If your misinterpretation has led you to quickly jump to a negative conclusion, your "I feel sad and no one likes me" theme just gained extra reinforcement. You just gave it more confirmation, regardless of whether it reflected the truth or not. This will now be improperly stored for further usage.

What causes this faulty thinking that makes us associate unrelated things? It could be that you have spent a long time throughout your life collecting false supportive interpretations. A theme can become addictive. In order to survive, it will begin to distort new information, just to keep itself alive. Certain negative feelings become especially hungry for support, and the more negative data it collects, the harder it becomes for us to break that cycle. So how do we resolve this problem? How do we unmask all the different beliefs that have been supporting our lingering emotions? This process seems complicated, doesn't it?

Thoughts, emotions, and beliefs are highly intertwined, and it would take only one single familiar stimulus from the environment to reactivate associated emotions. New information is constantly being assimilated to existing ones. I believe that, for this reason, many of us fail in our attempt to manage our negative automatic thinking. We try to reframe a thought surrounding a belief and feel better for a while, yet soon after, that same strong emotion resurfaces. This simply means that this negative emotion may be a common denominator to another group of beliefs aside from the one targeted, one which perhaps we have not yet discovered. That is why fixing just one piece of the equation may not produce lasting relief.

The ideal would be to unmask and explore all of our distorted thinking, elucidating all of the fragments stored to our belief systems, including subconscious beliefs. We would have to recall and analyze all of the related thoughts we have ever stored to memory. It would be a long process to locate all the fragments; it is not impossible of course and there are many wonderful ways of initiating that process. Yet, I needed something new, a strategy that would be all encompassing. I asked myself how I could acquire a new way of perceiving, of being and envisioning—but more importantly, how I could begin to stimulate and open up what is hidden in order to explore it further.

CHAPTER 7

About the Program:
Awareness and
Self-Discovery

I set out to construct a holistic platform that would invite you to an inner exploration, one that would allow for the possibility of improvements through all the various areas of your life. I believe that as we gather to introduce and practice new truths, the old programming begins to weaken. It is possible that by the simple practice of this exercise, you will begin to gain beautiful new insights; it will certainly help you gather strength. This will assist you in stimulating your mind to awaken the areas that may have remained dormant and neglected for so long.

How does it all work?

By bringing into awareness the multifaceted aspects that form the individual self, a process of deep self-discovery is initiated. Growth will begin to take place at a whole new level. You set off an intention of increasing communication within all parts of the self: thoughts, emotions, beliefs, and action.

This mental activity introduces a new set of precepts consisting of precisely chosen words. I specifically focused on words that carried a special purpose, words that could bring new meanings into my life. By meditating upon this foundation, many things can take place. You can be guided toward discovering your own sense of purpose in life. This happens as you redirect your energies within. As you speak each word out loud, you begin to refocus your attention on new possibilities, and so new expectations are created. You will gain strength in all areas by focusing on each one of them, and they will serve to motivate and encourage growth. While gaining new perspectives, the fear that has kept you motionless for so long will begin to slowly dissipate. The best part is that the new improvements will happen at your own individual pace.

The words that I have chosen hold the key to opening many doors. They actually channel meaning, abundance, prosperity, and success. Why did I choose these words? A single word can have both intrinsic and extrinsic value. Certainly, when they stand alone, each word carries an objective meaning—as a matter of fact we know that entire concepts can be represented by a single word. Not only can a single word have the power to ignite thousands and thousands of past memories, it can also have the power to ignite certain emotions. With words we can illustrate the perceptions of our current reality. They are also the building material of our thoughts, with power to add weakness or strength, to create an internal war or to cause inner peace. The choice of words unquestionably colors our thoughts and perceptions.

Now, if you will, imagine what would happen if you were used to a meek vocabulary, where everything you described was either good or bad, okay, or disastrous. Poor selection of words can mean poor descriptions to situations. Certainly, there are also serious implications of a deprived vocabulary, since that is what you will be using to illustrate your life experiences. If you have a habit of using only a few sets of words to describe all that you are experiencing, you may fall more easily into black and white thinking. Things will always be either good or bad and nothing in between.

It is interesting that the **promptness** of certain words is dependent upon practice and habit. This can influence us while we are in the act of perceiving and forming information, because your probability of word choice, such as a descriptive word, will also depend on this ability to keep those words readily available. The practice of a renewed vocabulary can aid in disrupting the regular, negative pathways by providing readily available and positive keywords for daily usage. Keywords can serve as prompts for constructive thinking. These words will also help you reflect and keep you continuously attuned to the various elements or areas of your life.

When we interrupt the disruptive pathways, negative thoughts are dislocated and with time inhibited from being recycled. Upon introduction and practice of this positive foundation, the new processes eventually become second nature. What we are creating here are supportive habits that will pose obstacles to old thought patterns.

I strongly believe that the negative programming previously

embedded in our minds is the main culprit of our negative thoughts. By increasing the number of constructive and positive words that are readily available, they will begin to show up with more frequency. This frequency increases the probability of retrieval during the process of forming new interpretations. Our objective here is to not only improve the content of your thoughts but to also make constructive thoughts more automatic. We are making new songs! We are also creating a foundation that will lead to new ways of thinking, with more awareness, discernment, clarity, and certainty.

As we introduce this positive platform, new productive thoughts will have a better chance of being constructed. But it is not just about concentrating on the positive; some of the words, as I have been mentioning, actually incorporate very precise meaning. Each individual word touches on the main subjects of our core values and beliefs and stimulate those areas toward positive changes.

This practice initiates you into the process of discovering fresh ways of being and envisioning. We must remember that what we put forth is what we have to draw from, and a supportive foundation will help you generate positive interpretations. This unique sequence does not keep focus on the reasons of why certain thoughts are not working; instead it redirects your focus to what could work, what is possible. It is present and future oriented. The contrast of where we are in our thinking to where we would like to be will bring about dynamic changes.

There is some truth, of course, that what we resist tends to continue and what we focus on tends to expand. This method can not only strengthen and enhance positive pathways, but it can also help you create new imprints. Furthermore, it encourages the most important part of the process of self-improvement, which is awareness.

Don't underestimate the incredible potential of your mind. What I have presented here will allow you to tap into that inner power to transform the self in ways in which you had never imagined before.

What I also found after practicing this technique is that, while I improved in one area, many other areas developed in relationship to it. As I brought focus to the word communication, I definitely became more aware of my own communication. It was a clear command that allowed me to reflect on it as I went about my day. Once I was attentive to it, I was capable of naturally making many developments in this area, and as a result, my relationships improved. When I repeatedly brought into focus the concepts of understanding and gratitude, my empathy increased alongside. With this foundation, many aspects of the self will be revisited so that those areas can be brought to light.

This mental training contains precepts that incorporate virtues, values, and a path to mastery. The central focus of this book is to provide a template that directs the individual into becoming mindful of the various essential elements of the self. If these are given proper attention, they will allow for greater advances. This template guides one into becoming an active observer and striving for improvements in all the areas. I don't want you to simply survive—I want you to really thrive!

Creating awareness, I repeat, is a major step toward change. We may discover that we have been neglecting many aspects of the self, or perhaps we never took the time to explore them. There are areas that that could have been overlooked and that are in desperate need for improvements. Perhaps you have taken yourself for granted all these years, but it is now time to embark in this wonderful journey of self-examination and personal growth. This journey could magnify your quality of life and well-being. As you get to know yourself, you may begin to better understand others. Taking this introspective stance will be the key to creating delightful changes in your life.

CHAPTER 8

Changing Our Outlook

> To make anything a habit, do it; to not make it a
> habit, do not do it; to unmake a habit, do something
> else in place of it.

> - Epictetus

I wanted to bring focus the topic of expectations. Nothing prompts our thoughts, emotions, and behavior as much as our expectations do. Our anticipations have a tremendous amount of influence in the manner in which we perceive reality. We are inclined to perceive what we expect to perceive. The declarative commands of this book have an incredible potential to become self-evident.

Through this mental activity, we are creating changes in our patterns of expectation. We are transferring power back to ourselves and our future realizations. Do not let the simplicity of this formula deceive you! Don't underestimate it! After some time, you will begin correlating new observations to your newly created platform. You will start harnessing extraordinary creativity to help you reach your full potential. With frequent use of this exercise, you will completely shift the energy that you bring into your life. You will be vibrating to new words and contacting the creative power inside. In little to no time, you will be creating new connections that can alter the way in which you perceive the world. You will begin to access and activate a whole new source of supply. Let it flow!

> If you wish to be an extraordinary person, if you
> wish to be wise, then you should explicitly identify
> the kind of person you aspire to become.

> - Epictetus

CHAPTER 9

The I Flow Method

The goal here is to create a three-word command that will be used before you speak each word from the main list. Follow these four simple steps.

Step 1: Choose one word or phrase from the list below. (This will be the first part of your sentence.)

- God
- Universal power
- Universe
- Creator
- Source
- Divine center
- Divine provider
- Life
- Nature

Step 2: Choose a word or phrase from the list below. (This will be used as a second part of your sentence.)

- Bless me with
- Give me
- Bring me
- Grant me
- Reveal to me
- Grant me with
- Impart in me
- Fill me with

If you feel more comfortable with a different format, you can skip steps 1 and 2 and use the following instead.

- I flow with

Step 3: Choose a word or phrase from the list below. (This will form the third part of your sentence. This will describe the level of updating that you would like to accomplish.)

- Divine and perfect
- Extraordinary
- Elevated
- Superior
- Advanced
- Amplified
- Heightened
- Optimum
- Unrivaled
- Supreme
- Exceptional
- Maximum
- Highest
- Surpassing
- Unlimited
- Uninterrupted

Step 4: Before you begin reading the list of words, below are some samples of my own, from the steps above.

- God bless me with divine and perfect ... abilities, ability to aver ... ability to evince and so on...
- I flow with exceptional ... abilities, ability to aver...

You may repeat this initial sentence in front of each single word, or you may use it in the beginning only and follow with the main list.

A

abilities, ability to aver, ability to evince, ability to see, ability to envision, ability to notice, abreaction, abstract intelligence, abundance, acceptance, acceptance of love, accessibility, accurateness, accuracy, achievements, accomplishments, accord, accountability, acknowledgements, actions, activations, activities, actualizations, acumen, adaptability, adjustments, advances, advancements, advantages, affect, affections, affiliations, affinity, affirmations, affluence, agility, agreements, alchemy, alertness, alliances, alignment, allocations, alternatives, altruism, ambitions, amorousness, analogies, analysis, anointing, announcements, answers, appreciation, appreciativeness, approachability, approaches, aptitude, ardor, articulation, artistic abilities, ascension, aspirations, assertiveness, assessments, assimilations, assistance, associations, assurance, astute, attainments, attention, attentiveness, attendance, attitude, attraction, attributes, attunement, audacity, aura, authority, availability, awareness, awe

B

balance, beauty, beginnings, behavior, beliefs, benevolence, boldness, boundaries, bountifulness, bravery, breathing, breakthroughs, brilliance

C

calculations, calmness, career, carefreeness, cares, catharsis, causation, cause, celebrations, centering, changes, character, charm, charisma, cheerfulness, choices, circumstances, clarity, clearance of negativity, cleverness, closeness, codes, coexistence, cognitions, collaborations, confirmations, contributions, command comfort, commemorations, comments, commitments, common sense, communication, companionship, compassion, competence, completions, composure, comprehensiveness, concentration, concepts, conceptions, consistency, concretization, confidence, congruency, connections, consent, considerations, consolation, consonance, constancy, contemplations, content, context, continuation, continuity, contracts, contributions, conversations, conviction, coordination, cooperation, cordiality, corrections, correlations, consciousness, counsel, courage, courtesy, creations, creativity, credibility, cultural awareness, curiosity

D

decency, decisions, decisiveness, declarations, deeds, deductions, deliverance, demeanor, demonstration, dependability, design, desires, details, determination, development, devotion, digestion, dignity, diligence, diplomacy, direction, discernment, discipline, disclosures, discoveries, discretion, dispositions, doctrines, dreams, dream revelations

E

eagerness, education, effectiveness, efficiency, efforts, elegance, elements, eloquence, emotional balance, emotional stability, emotional support, emotions, empathy, empowerment, enchantment, encounters, endeavors, encouragement, endorsements, endowment, endurance, energy, engagements, enjoyment, enterprises, enthusiasm, intonation, environment, equilibrium, essence, essentiality, estimations, ethics, evaluations, events, evolution, exactness, examples, exchanges, existence, expansion, experiences, expertise, explorations, expressions

F

facts, faith, fair-mindedness, fairness, family, familiarity, favors, fearlessness, feedback, fervor, finances, findings, firmness, flexibility, flow, focus, foresight, forgiveness, foreknowledge, forethoughts, form, formulas, fortitude, freedom, free will, frequencies, friendships, fruitfulness, fulfilments, fun, functioning, future

G

gains, generosity, genius, genuineness, gentleness, gestures, gifts, giving, gladness, goals, good habits, goodness, grace, gratefulness, gratification, greatness, gratitude, growth, guidance

H

habits, happiness, harmony, healing, health, help, helpfulness, honesty, honor, hope, hospitality, humbleness, humility, humor

I

ideas, identifications, identity, independence, illumination, images, imagination, immunity, impartiality, importance, impressions, improvements, inclinations, inclusion, increases, independence, inferences, inflow, influence, information, initiative, inner-peace, input, insight, inspiration, instinct, introspective, instruction, integration, integrity, intellect, intelligence, intent, intentions, interactions, interconnectedness, interests, internal peace, internal dialogue, interpretations, interventions, intimacy, intuition, inventiveness, investments, involvement, inward-looking

J

joy, jubilee, judgment, justice

K

kindness, knowledge

L

laughs, leadership, leisure, learning, leeway, lessons, letting go, level-headedness, life force, lightness, likings, listening, liveliness, location, logic, longevity, unconditional love, loyalty

M

magnetism, magnificence, manifestations, manners, mastery, material goods, materialization, maturity, meaning, memory, mental efficacy, mental acuteness, mental accurateness, mental capacity, mental clarity, mental energy, mental quickness, mental processes, merit, mind, mindfulness, mind over matter, miracles, moderation, modesty, momentum, mood, morale, morals, motivations, movements

N

nature, networks, necessities, needs, notions, nourishment, nurturing, nutrition

O

objectives, objectivity, observations, oneness, openness, opinions, opportunities, optimism, optimization, options, order, orderliness, organization, orientation, originality, output

P

participation, partner, patterns, passion, patience, peace, peace of mind, perceptions, percepts precepts, performances, persuasiveness, philosophies, physiology, picturing, place, plans, planning, playfulness, pleasure, pledges, plentitude, politeness, positivity, postulates, power, power to assuage, power to will, practicality, praises, prayers, precision, precognition, premonition, preparation, presence, preservation, principles, priorities, privilege, proactivity, problem-solving, productivity, prophecy, profit, proficiency, programming, progress, prompts, prosperity, protection, providence, provisions, prudence, punctuality, purpose, purity, pursuits

Q

qualities, qualifications, questions, quests, quickness

R

radiance, rationality, reactions, readings, readiness, reality, realizations, reasoning, reasons, receptiveness, reconciliations, recollections, reckoning, regards, refinement, reflections, reflectiveness, reflexes, relatedness, relaxation, reliability, release, relief, renewal, self-renewal, requests, repentance, replies, resilience, respect, resonance, resources, resourcefulness, responses, responsiveness, rest, restoration, results, retrieval, memory-retrieval, revelations, reverence, revitalization, rewards, richness, romance

S

safety, salience, satisfaction, science, searches, self-approval, self-awareness, self-assurance, self-care, self-concept, self-control, self-command, self-care, self-determination, self-discipline, self-disclosure, self-discovery, self-esteem, self-image, self-identification, self-expression, self-consistency, self-discovery, self-forgiveness, self-governance, self-initiative, self-mastery, self-possession, self-preservation, self-realization, self-regard, selflessness, self-sufficient, sensibility, sensitivity, sentience, serenity, sharing, sharpness,

sharpness of senses, sharpness of the memory, sharpness of the mind, sense of belonging, sight, signs, signals, silence, simplicity, skills, sociability, solace, solutions, soul-searching, source, sources, speech, speed, splendor, stability, standards, strength, spirituality, successes, suggestions, supply, support, surplus, survival, sweetness, symbology, synchronization, synergy

T

tact, talents, teaching, temperament, temperance, tenacity, tenderness, thankfulness, theories, thoughts, thoughtfulness, time, tolerance, tone, transcendence, tranquility, transformations, translations, travels, treasures, triumphs, thoroughness, trust, trustworthiness, truth

U

unassuming attitude, unconditional love, understanding, undertakings, unity, upholding, uplifting

V

validity, validation, values, vibrance, victory, viewpoints, vigor, virtues, visions, vitality, visualizations, voice, vocalization

W

wakefulness, warmth, wealth, well-being, wellness, wholesomeness, will, willpower, willingness, wisdom, words, work, worth, writings

Y

youthfulness

Z

zeal, Zen, zest

I believe that as you begin practicing, you will be encoding a new system, and your thoughts and emotions will begin to shift. This is a powerful tool that you can use to really look within and apply mindful attention to the various parts of the self. This foundation can enhance your mental and emotional abilities. It is a mental discipline that will be bringing new order and more congruency into your life. It is about taking a step forward, moving away from feeling stuck. It is also about switching your intentionality to motivate your emotions and behavior. My hope for you is that you begin experiencing more clarity, joy, love, well-being, and prosperity in your life.

> What matters most is what sort of person you are becoming. Wise individuals care only about whom they are today and who they can be tomorrow.
>
> - Epictetus

ABOUT THE AUTHOR

Flavia Mosci enjoys celebrating different cultures. She is a citizen of Brazil, Italy, and the United States. Her research interests are in the areas of Child Psychology, Spirituality & Mental Health, Consciousness and Wellness. She holds a BSC in Finance from Florida State University and a Master of Science in Counseling Psychology from Troy University. She is now looking forward to begging a PHD program in Clinical Psychology. At the present, she is working by providing mental health counseling to foster care kids in the state of Florida, where she resides. In her free time, she enjoys traveling, reading, belly-dancing, practicing kundalini yoga, beach walks and nature walks, gardening, and cooking.

Printed in the United States
By Bookmasters